My Great Big Pig

A True Story

written and illustrated by:
Kaleigh LeBeau

and he was round.

He flashed a BIG smile while he sniffed the ground.

and called for him to come.

I did not know a pig so BIG could RUN!

He came up to our house and had a nice snack.

In loving memory of our greatest, biggest pig, Ferdinand.

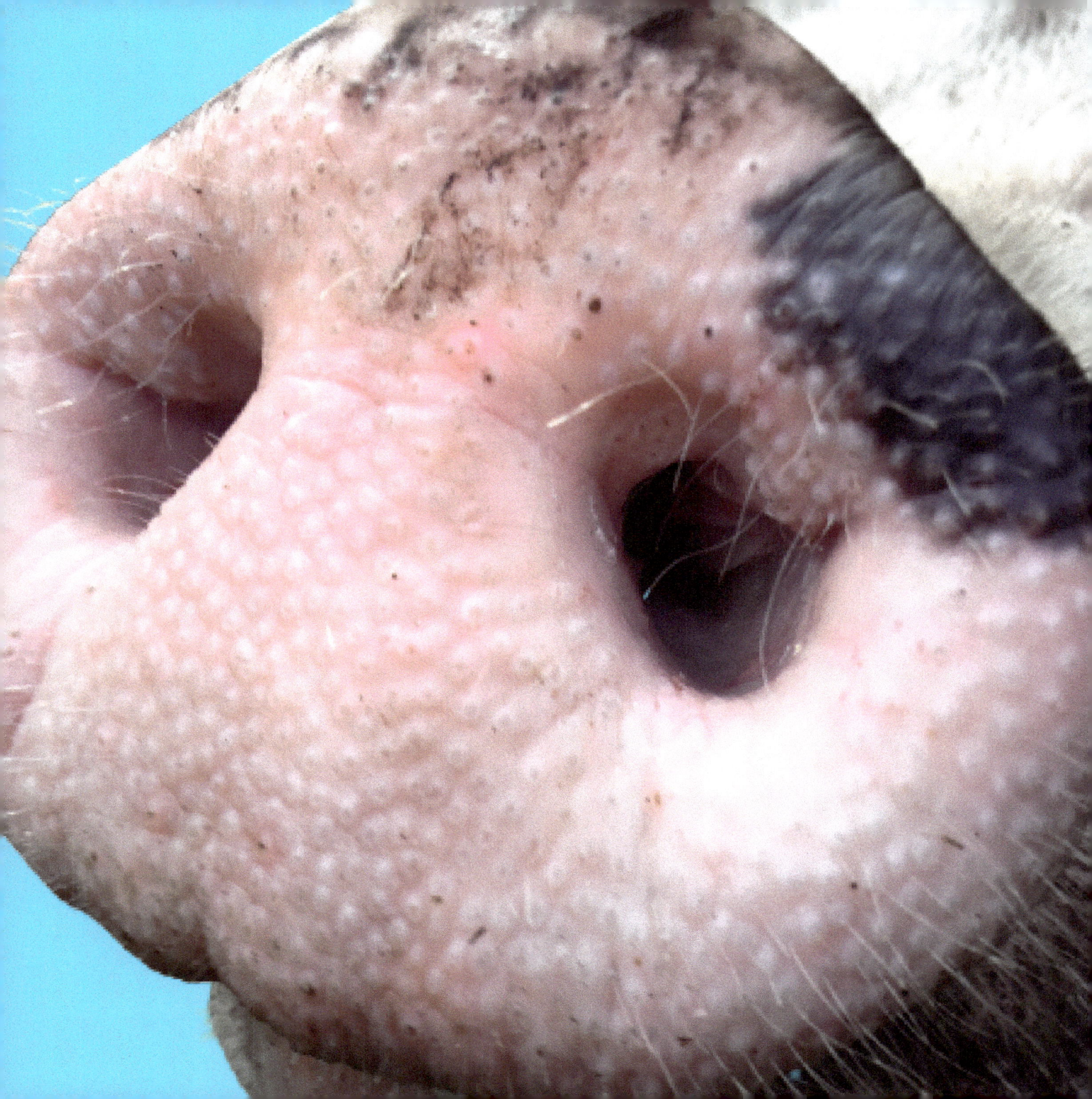

www.ingramcontent.com/pod-product-compliance
Lightning Source LLC
Chambersburg PA
CBHW061801290426
44109CB00030B/2918